Puffle Whisperer

PH's Puffle Handbook

9030 00002 9027 1

SUNBIRD
PENGUIN

Published by Ladybird Books Ltd 2012
A Penguin Company

Penguin Books Ltd, 80 Strand,
London WC2R 0RL, UK
Penguin Group Australia Ltd, 250 Camberwell Road,
Camberwell, Victoria 3124, Australia
Penguin Group (NZ), 67 Apollo Drive, Rosedale,
North Shore 0632, New Zealand
(a division of Pearson New Zealand Ltd)

All rights reserved. No part of this publication may be reproduced, stored in
a retrieval system, or transmitted in any form or by any means, electronic,
mechanical, photocopying, recording or otherwise, without the prior
consent of the copyright owner.

www.ladybird.com
ISBN: 9781409391074

10 9 8 7 6 5 4 3 2 1
Printed in Slovakia

Dear Puffle Fans,

Welcome! My name is PH and this is my guide to puffles – incredible little pets that can be adopted in Club Penguin. Some call me the biggest puffle fan of them all, and they're right! I am devoted to all things puffle. I wanted to write a book to share my love and knowledge of puffles with other puffle fans.

I spend a lot of time exploring the wilderness and studying puffles. I go where the puffles are – no matter how far I must travel. I've learned heaps along the way and I'll share what I know with you in this book.

Get ready to learn about my favourite creatures. You'll learn how to adopt and care for all types of puffles. I'll also share puffle trivia and history And, when you're done, you'll be a puffle expert too!

PH

Table of Contents

How to Adopt Puffles

Now you know all about me and my love of puffles! You don't just have to watch them from a distance in the wild. Thanks to the Pet Shop, you can adopt puffles and take them home to live in your igloo. The Pet Shop is in The Plaza, next to The Stage. Here's how to do it:

What You'll Need

It costs 800 coins to adopt a puffle. Everyone can adopt up to two puffles: blue or red. Members can adopt up to twenty puffles in ten different colours: blue, red, pink, black, green, purple, yellow, white, orange and brown.

Picking the Perfect Puffle

There are ten types of puffles, and each colour puffle has its own unique personality. To find the perfect puffle for you, click on the puffles in the left-hand corner of the Pet Shop, under the sign that says 'Adopt a Puffle'. Click on the quiz: 'Which puffle is the most like you?' Answer the questions and you'll be matched with the puffle that is most like you. You can choose to adopt that puffle, or a different one. It is up to you!

Do a little research of your own by reading the 'Puffle Handbook'. It's the purple book next to the puffles, and yes, it was written by me! Click on it to learn all about the different puffle types.

When you adopt a puffle, you have to name it. Choose the name carefully. Once you pick a name, you can't change it.

Be a Good Owner

Your puffle will trust you to take care of it. Puffles need to be fed, bathed, taken for walks and played with. If you don't take care of your puffle, it might run away to the wild!

When you log out of Club Penguin, your puffle won't get tired or hungry, so you don't have to worry while you are not playing.

The Pet Shop

The Pet Shop is where you can adopt puffles. But that's just the start of the fun you can have here!

Games Galore

Play Pufflescape, Puffle Launch and Puffle Roundup! You can earn coins while exercising your pet.

Do Some Shopping

Keep your puffle happy and healthy with the food, toys, houses, beds and hats you can buy from the Puffle Catalog:

Toys: When you buy a toy for your puffle, it gets added to your igloo storage. Put it in your igloo to watch your puffle play with it.

Super Toys: Each colour of puffle will only play with its own super toy. When you play with your puffle, drag the super toy to it. Don't buy a purple puffle's disco ball for your red puffle - it won't play with it!

Houses: Give your puffle a comfy spot to relax in your igloo. Houses are also added to your igloo storage.

Bedzzz: Puffles like a soft spot to snooze. Like houses and regular toys, it will be added to your igloo storage.

Food: Stock up on snacks like pizza, cookies, carrots, bubble gum and Puffle O's for your puffles.

Puffle Hats: Dress your puffles in pirate hats, princess caps, jester hats and more!

Did You Know?

If you walk your puffle into the Pet Shop, the rug in the middle of the floor will change colour to match your puffle! Don't believe me? Try it yourself!

The Pet Shop first opened in March 2006. Later, I was asked to redesign it, and I agreed. Of course, I couldn't have done it without the help of some trusty puffles. They helped me make the changes, and in March 2011 the new Pet Shop look was complete.

During the Medieval Party, the Pet Shop is changed into a stable. Check back during other parties, too. It often gets some cool decorations!

Let's Time Travel!

No matter how much I discover about puffles, there is always more to learn! For instance, nobody really knows the history of puffles. I'll keep searching for answers. In the meantime, I have fun imagining what puffles may have been like in different periods of history.

Let's take a trip through the years and see what puffles may have been up to.

Prehistoric Times

Fire!

Before early
penguins
discovered fire,
there was no pizza
to eat; only cold
fish and seaweed. Did
black puffles help cave penguins
discover fire? Then they'd be warming their flippers over the
hot flames in no time!

Ice Age

White puffles would have loved living in the Ice Age. Back
then, the whole world was one big, slippery ice rink!

Ancient Egypt

Built for Speed

We know that the pyramids were built as tombs for ancient kings. I bet black puffles would have found another use for them. The smooth sloping sides of a pyramid make it the ultimate skate park!

Puffles and Papyrus

Yellow puffles might have invented their own hieroglyphs to tell their own amazing tales.

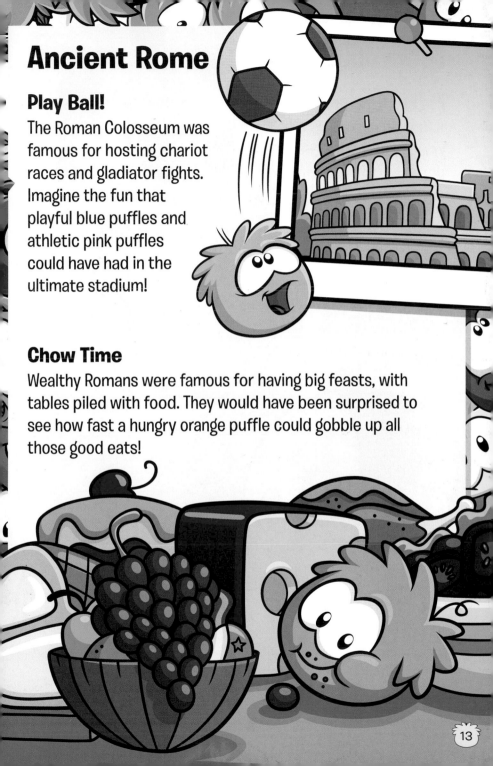

Ancient Rome

Play Ball!

The Roman Colosseum was famous for hosting chariot races and gladiator fights. Imagine the fun that playful blue puffles and athletic pink puffles could have had in the ultimate stadium!

Chow Time

Wealthy Romans were famous for having big feasts, with tables piled with food. They would have been surprised to see how fast a hungry orange puffle could gobble up all those good eats!

Medieval Times

Highly Amusing

A fun-loving green puffle would have made the perfect court jester for any king or queen.

Powerful Protection

Medieval castles were often under attack from invaders. Cannons filled with red puffles would have been a great defence against any enemy!

The Renaissance

True Genius

Leonardo da Vinci is thought to be one of the greatest inventors of all time. Who knows? Maybe he had a brown puffle as his assistant.

Ballet is Born

Purple puffles love all kinds of dancing. They would certainly have joined the very first ballet dancers as they twirled and spun across the stage. Although they might have had one problem – how do you get a tutu on a puffle?

The Great Puffle Discovery

Can you imagine Club Penguin without puffles? Once upon a time, it was a reality. I know it's very hard to imagine – but it's true! Penguins used to be puffle-less. Until November 2005 that is, when small, furry creatures were spotted near the Snow Forts.

A team of penguin scientists investigated. They found out that the creatures were animals that lived in the wilds of Club Penguin. The scientists also learned that they are very friendly.

Penguins were asked to help round up these sweet creatures. And, in true Club Penguin style, everyone rushed to help. But what were we going to call these new critters? A contest was held, and penguins submitted over one thousand name ideas! As we all know, the name 'puffles' won.

The first puffle colours discovered were blue, pink, green and black. Soon after that, penguins were able to adopt them and keep them in their igloos.

Eventually, purple, red, yellow, white, orange and brown puffles were found. What other puffles are hidden in the wilds, waiting to be discovered? We can only imagine. I'll always be on the look-out for new ones!

How to Care for Blue Puffles

Adopt a blue puffle, and you'll have a true blue friend for life! These friendly puffles are very loyal and are known for their awesome teamwork. Since they are so easy-going, they are among the easiest puffles to care for.

The key to taking good care of a blue puffle is to be best friends with it!

Feeding Blue Puffles

Pour the milk and get out the cookies! Since your blue puffle is so nice it won't mind sharing its favourite snack with you.

Play Time!

When you play with your blue puffle, you'll discover it already owns its very own ball. Watch it kick it around your igloo!

To see your blue puffle do a cool trick, buy it the bouncy ball from the Puffle Catalog. It'll bounce the ball on its head before balancing it on its nose!

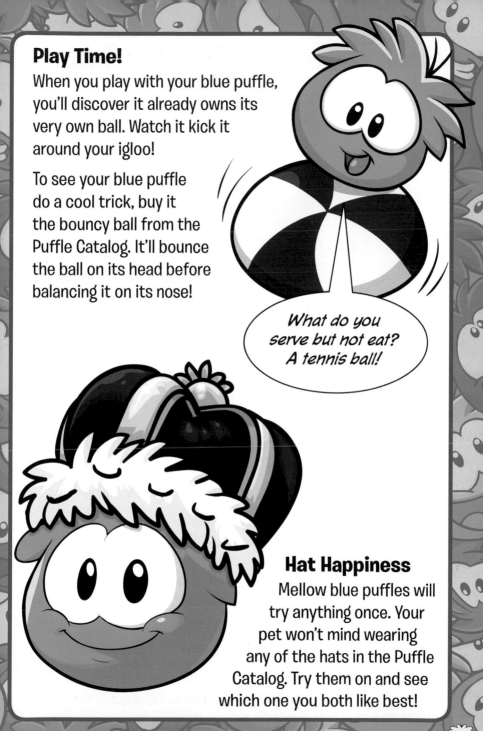

What do you serve but not eat? A tennis ball!

Hat Happiness

Mellow blue puffles will try anything once. Your pet won't mind wearing any of the hats in the Puffle Catalog. Try them on and see which one you both like best!

How to Care for Pink Puffles

The key to taking good care of a pink puffle is making sure it stays active.

Pink puffles make cheery companions. But if you want to be a pink puffle owner, you've got to keep up with your pet! Pink puffles are great athletes who love to exercise and swim. They are also good sports and are always smiling, win or lose!

Feeding Pink Puffles

Pink puffles like to be in tip-top shape, so they like to eat foods that are good for them. You can find carrots and Puffle O's in the Puffle Catalog. Feed them to your pink puffle to keep it healthy and happy!

Your pink puffle does enjoy a treat from time to time. Give it a piece of bubble gum. It likes to blow bubbles and float!

Play Time!

You can buy furniture in the Puffle Catalog to add to your igloo. Your pink puffle will enjoy more active toys, like the Running Wheel. Pick out furniture that will keep your pink puffle moving!

Treat your pink puffle to a special toy! Your pink puffle will come with its very own jump rope. Your active puffle will love playing with it. Want to spoil your pet even more? Shop the Super Toys section in the Puffle Catalog for the trampoline. It will have a ball bouncing up and down on it!

Hat Happiness

Puffles like expressing themselves through clothes just like penguins do! That's why the Pet Shop now includes clothing for puffles. Pink puffles will especially enjoy the headphones. They can listen to music while exercising!

What time of year do you jump on a trampoline? Spring time!

Game Spotlight: Aqua Grabber

Your pink puffle can come along with you on an undersea adventure in the mini game Aqua Grabber! Take your pink puffle for a walk to the Iceberg. Play Aqua Grabber and your pink pet will appear in the game with you wearing scuba gear. It'll swim alongside you as you search for treasure.

Playing Aqua Grabber with your pink puffle can help you earn more coins!

How to Play

Take Control

To explore the ocean and collect treasure, you'll need to move the Aqua Grabber around. Use the arrow keys to move up, down, left and right. Press the spacebar to pick up treasure or to drop something.

Pearls of Wisdom

Wait until the blue oyster falls asleep before grabbing the pearl.

Treasure Galore!

You'll find lots of treasure on the ocean floor. Small items fit right on the Aqua Grabber. But big items need to be brought to the net.

Breathe Easy

If you run out of air, you lose a turn. Move over large air bubbles - they will give you extra oxygen. You can also get air by going above the surface of the water.

Stamp Book

Your pink puffle can help you earn Aqua Grabber Stamps!

Aqua Puffle

Take your pink puffle for a deep-sea dive by playing Aqua Grabber to earn this Stamp!

Bubble Catch

To earn this ⬡ ⬡ ⬡ collect a bubble from y⬡ ⬡ ⬡ ⬡.

How to Care for Green Puffles

Do you like to laugh? If you adopt a green puffle, you might never stop! These playful and funny puffles like to keep their owners smiling. If you've got a good sense of humour, you'll get along great with this pet.

Feeding Green Puffles

Green puffles like snacks that match their personality - silly! If you can't find candy, try cookies or pizza.

Play Time!

Did you know that when you adopt your green puffle, it will come with its very own unicycle? And it sure knows how to ride! You'll be impressed with how well your green puffle can play with it.

To further the fun, buy the green puffle's propeller cap from the Puffle Catalog. Let your pet play with it and watch it zoom through the air!

Why can unicyclists always ride longer than bicyclists? Because bicyclists are always TWO tired!

Hat Happiness

Your green puffle can wear the propeller cap ALL the time, not just when it's playing with it. Buy a cap from the Puffle Catalog to keep your green puffle grinning. Or try the jester hat. It's a perfect fit for a green puffle's funny personality.

The key to taking good care of a green puffle is to always laugh along with it!

Game Spotlight:
Jet Pack Adventure

Fly high with your green puffle, and collect coins in the skies above Club Penguin in the mini game Jet Pack Adventure! Take your green puffle for a walk to the Lighthouse. Climb up to the Beacon and play Jet Pack Adventure. Your green puffle will fly alongside you in its propeller cap.

Playing Jet Pack Adventure with your green puffle can help you earn more coins!

How to Play

Flight Plan

Using your arrow keys, soar through the skies and fly into coins, fuel and extra jet packs. Avoid coffee bags and anvils. Crashing into them will make you run out of fuel faster.

Look Out Below!

Only land on the designated landing pads at the end of each level. If you run out of jet packs, you'll parachute safely to the ground.

Stamp Book

Your green puffle can help you earn Jet Pack Adventure Stamps!

Puffle Pilot
Bring your green puffle into the game to earn this Stamp.

Puffle Bonus
Your green puffle collects 200 coins.

Puffle Plus
Your green puffle collects 450 coins.

Puffle Boost
Your green puffle gets a gas can when you run out of fuel.

How to Care for Black Puffles

Black puffles aren't exactly what they seem. At first glance, they look like they'd make mellow pets. But every once in a while they have a sudden burst of energy and erupt into flames! If you can handle that, you'll get along great with a black puffle. They are known as the strong, silent puffles.

Feeding Black Puffles

Black puffles act like they don't care about what they eat. But their favourite snack is chips!

The key to taking good care of a black puffle is letting it have its own space.

Play Time!

When you adopt your black puffle, it will
come with its very own skateboard.
Playing with its skateboard will
get it to smile, something that
doesn't happen a lot. Black
puffles love to skate and are
really good at it.

To watch your normally grumpy
black puffle erupt into fiery flames,
buy it the black puffle's hot sauce from the Puffle Catalog.
Stand back when you let your pet play with it!

Hat Happiness

Black puffles act so cool sometimes; it's hard to tell
what they're thinking. But I've observed they really like to
wear hats, even if they don't let on.
Headphones will let your black puffle
listen to music while
it plays. Or try the
crown. After all, this
puffle is the king of
skateboarding!

*What did the banana say when the
black puffle skateboarded over it?
Nothing! Bananas don't talk.*

Game Spotlight: Cart Surfer

Take a wild ride on a mine cart with your black puffle in the mini game Cart Surfer! Walk your black puffle to the Mine. Play Cart Surfer and your pet will appear in the game. It will ride in the cart and even do tricks with you!

Playing Cart Surfer with your black puffle can help you earn extra coins!

How to Play
Balancing Act
As you ride through the mine at top speeds, you have to try not to tip over. This gets tricky. Especially when the track turns. Lean into it or you'll crash!

Be a Trickster
Score big by doing tricks. Press the spacebar to jump and press the up and down arrows to try different moves. But don't try to do a trick while turning or you will crash. The more tricks you and your puffle do, the more you'll earn.

Stamp Book
Your black puffle can help you earn Cart Surfer Stamps!

Puffle Power
Recover from a wobble with your black puffle alongside you to earn this Stamp.

Ultimate Duo
Perform 20 tricks with your puffle.

How to Care for Purple Puffles

These stylish puffles enjoy the finer things in life. If you want to be a purple puffle owner, you've got to spoil this picky pet. And you've got to love to dance. A purple puffle will bust a move, anytime, anywhere - and it will want you to dance along with it!

Feeding Purple Puffles

Purple puffles are very picky eaters. Its favourite snack is very expensive chocolate. Sometimes when you feed it, it won't eat right away!

The key to taking good care of a purple puffle is spoiling it!

Play Time!

You can buy furniture in the Puffle Catalog to add to your igloo. Spoil your fussy pet with a salon chair - it loves to be pampered!

Your pet puffle will come with its very own bubble wand. It will blow bubbles when it plays. If you want to know how, you'll need the disco ball in the Super Toys section of the Puffle Catalog. A purple puffle's favourite thing to do is dance!

Why don't dogs make good dancers? Because they have two left feet!

Hat Happiness

Purple puffles are known to be very stylish dressers. They always know how to choose just the right outfit for just the right occasion! These puffles enjoy being treated like royalty, so buy the Princess Cap or the Tiara from the Puffle Catalog. They'll love wearing them!

Turn to page 74 to find out how to make a Princess Cap of your very own!

Game Spotlight: Dance Contest

Move to the beat with your purple puffle and earn coins when you play Dance Contest at the Night Club! Take your purple puffle for a walk to the Town Centre and waddle into the Night Club. Look for the Dance Contest poster to start playing. Your purple puffle will dance alongside you.

How to Play

Fast Fingers

Match the arrow to follow the dance steps. When the coloured arrows line up with the gray arrows at the top left of your screen, press the matching arrow key on your keyboard. Hold down the key during long arrows for a score bonus. Hit a bunch of arrows correctly in a row to get a combo bonus. You'll earn more coins!

Take it Slow

Cadence (the greatest dancer I know!) will show you how it's done when you choose the "How to Play" option. After you get your dance lesson, start with "Easy" and work your way up to "Hard."

Bring on the Competition!

You can dance solo or share the floor with other penguins in Dance Contest. Choose "Multiplayer" to go head to head with another penguin dancer.

How to Care for Red Puffles

When you adopt a red puffle, adventure awaits! There is never a dull moment around these action-loving puffles. They love thrilling sports, like surfing. If you're up for a challenge, you'll love trying to keep up with a red puffle!

Feeding Red Puffles

Since they are always going from one adventure to the next, red puffles aren't fussy about what they eat. They're daredevils and they like trying new food. Like Rockhopper, they're big fans of pizza and stinky cheese!

What is the best type of ship? FriendSHIP!

Play Time

Red puffles love to bowl! In fact, when you adopt one, it will come with its very own bowling pins.

But bowling isn't enough for this adventurous puffle. Buy the cannon from the Puffle Catalog. Your daring red puffle will love blasting out of it!

Hat Happiness

Hold on to your hats - the bold red puffle loves to search for adventure. Dress it in a hat that reflects that and buy the Pirate Hat from the Puffle Catalog. Your red puffle will love it!

The key to taking good care of a red puffle is to never let it get bored.

Game Spotlight: Catchin' Waves

You can surf alongside your red puffle in the mini game Catchin' Waves! Head over to the Cove and go to the Surf Hut to get started.

How to Play:
Practice Makes Perfect
You'll need to practise to be a good surfer, so don't give up! You may wipe out a few times before you get the hang of it.

Surf Lesson
If it's your first time, take the surf lesson to learn how to play. After your lesson you can practice in Freestyle mode. Once you've mastered Freestyle, move on to Competition and Survival.

Hang Ten
Use your mouse to steer up and down, lean forward and back, and keep your balance. Use your keyboard to perform tricks. Press either the W, A, S, and D keys or the arrow keys while you are surfing. Try pressing different combination of keys to perform advanced tricks. The more tricks you do, the more coins you will earn!

Playing Catchin' Waves with your red puffle can help you earn more coins.

Stamp Book

Your red puffle can help you earn Catchin' Waves Stamps!

Puffle Surfin'
Take your red puffle for a surf lesson to earn this Stamp!

Podium Puffle
Finish in first, second or third place with your puffle.

How to Care for Yellow Puffles

From painting to acting to singing, yellow puffles are true artists. These creative creatures are always working on a new project - whether it's writing a song or sculpting. If you are an artist, too, you'll love to dream up new creations with a yellow puffle.

Feeding Yellow Puffles

These dreamy puffles sometimes get so lost in their art, they forget to eat! You'll have to remind them. While they particularly love to snack on cheese and crackers, yellow puffles aren't fussy and will enjoy most foods.

The key to taking good care of a yellow puffle is to let it express itself.

Play Time!

When you adopt your yellow puffle, it will come with its own paintbrush and paints. It's fun to watch it paint and see what masterpieces it creates. It might even paint a picture of you!

Let your yellow puffle direct its own movie. Buy it the Director's Chair and Camera from the Puffle Catalog to get it started.

Hat Happiness

Since yellow puffles always are looking for inspiration, buy the headphones from the Puffle Catalog to keep their creative juices flowing. This artistic puffle loves music, too, so it's a great pick!

What do you get when you mix a puffle and chocolate? Truffles!

Game Spotlight: DJ3K

Make some music with your puffle while you earn coins in the mini game DJ3K!

Take your yellow puffle for a walk to the Night Club. Head to the DJ table and click on the speakers to get grooving!

How to Play
Mix Master
Mix, match and scratch using the two turntables to create your own original song. There is no right or wrong way to play. Just have fun!

Click Away!
Explore the DJ equipment by clicking the different buttons and levers to discover what sounds they create. When you and your puffle start dancing, you'll know you've got a good groove going.

Listen in Your Igloo
Click the "Record" button to make a copy of your song. If you like it, you can save your song and name. You and your yellow puffle can enjoy the song you made together in your igloo if you own a jukebox or stereo!

How to Care for White Puffles

These shy pets may be smaller than other puffles. But don't confuse size with strength - these gentle puffles are actually quite powerful! They also love the cold weather and everything that comes with it.

Feeding White Puffles

White puffles love the cold and enjoy frozen snacks. I've observed, that with one blow of their icy breath, they can freeze their food! Watch what happens when you give one a piece of bubble gum.

Play Time!

All a white puffle needs to play is snow! Luckily, this little creature can make its own snow by using its breath.

Its powerful breath can also create an ice skating rink. Buy your white puffle the skate from the Puffle Catalog to watch it skate like an Olympic champ!

Hat Happiness

It's hard to imagine white puffles being any cuter, but try a hat from the Puffle Catalog. The Candy Cane Cap looks especially sweet on these little guys.

The key to taking good care of a white puffle is to give it a peaceful home.

What type of ball doesn't bounce? A snowball!

How to Care for Orange Puffles

It's hard not to notice an orange puffle. Their off-the-wall, high-energy antics get them attention. If you don't mind a lot of excitement, you'll get along great with this pet.

Feeding Orange Puffles

Orange puffles eat EVERYTHING! Even their puffle bowls. Instead of worrying about picking the perfect snack for your pet, you'll have to worry about it chewing up your furniture instead.

Play Time!

These zany puffles are very curious. They'll get into everything if they get bored. Be sure to give your pet plenty of play time. When you adopt your orange puffle, it will come with its own hula hoop. The only problem is, it likes to eat its hula hoop when it is done playing with it!

To really keep your orange puffle busy, buy it the orange puffle wagon from the Puffle Catalog. It's fun to watch it zoom around your igloo!

Hat Happiness

It's hard to take a silly orange puffle seriously. Help it express its wacky personality with a funny hat! The Jester Hat, Sombrero, and Squid Lid are all good picks for this pet.

> **The key to taking good care of an orange puffle is being up for anything!**

> *What can an orange puffle never eat for breakfast? Lunch and dinner!*

How to Care for Brown Puffles

Super-smart brown puffles make great pets! If you enjoy science and maths, you'll love having a brown puffle keep you company in your igloo. You'll never know what it's going to invent next!

Feeding Brown Puffles

Brown puffles are always busy working on their latest invention. In fact, they even dream about maths problems while they sleep! As their owner, you have to make sure they take a break and eat. These science-minded puffles love astronaut food, especially dehydrated ice cream sandwiches, but since those are hard to find on the island, they enjoy eating chocolate chip cookies, too. In fact, brown puffles invented a special ray to make cookies bigger.

The key to taking good care of a brown puffle is to allow it to experiment and invent new creations!

Play Time!

An ordinary ball won't do for these smart puffles. They come with their very own plasma ball. It makes their fur stand on end!

Buy your brown puffle the rocket from the Puffle Catalog. But be prepared for a crash landing! Did you know your brown puffle will put on its goggles, a helmet and a parachute before it zooms around your igloo?

Hat Happiness

What's the best hat for a puffle who likes to tinker with gadgets? The gear hat! It's a perfect fit for a brown puffle's inventive personality.

What do you call a puffle with a cold? A snuffle!

Game Spotlight: Pufflescape

Choose Orange

Puffles love to roll around in their exercise balls, so I helped to create the Pufflescape game to keep puffles happy and active. In this game, you guide your puffle through icy landscapes collecting Puffle O's and keys.

How to Play
Choose Your Puffle
You can choose any one of our own puffles to play the game. If you don't have a puffle, you can play with a white puffle.

Get Rolling
Use your arrow keys to roll your puffle through the landscape. Use your mouse key to move objects in the landscape so that you can get to hard-to-reach items.

Collect Puffle O's and Keys
Roll over any Puffle O to collect it. Once you get one Puffle O, a white box will appear. Click on it and you can get hints for that level. Roll over the key to open the gate that leads to the next level.

Go Extreme

If you collect all of the Puffle O's in a level, you can play the Extreme version of that level. It's the same level, but it's timed so you have to complete it quickly to succeed.

Tip: When you're first starting this game, go slow! There's no rush to finish a level, so take your time and try to get all of the Puffle O's.

Stamp Book

Eat Up!
You can earn five different Stamps by eating Puffle O's. The first one is easy—just eat one bonus Puffle O.

Master Levels
Earn a Stamp by completing levels 4, 8, 12, 17, 22, and 23.

Game Spotlight: Puffle Launch

This game was inspired by red puffles, who love to launch themselves out of cannons and soar through the air. But you can play with any of your own puffles. Just head to the Pet Shop and click on the big red cannon to get started.

How to Play
Blast Off!
You can choose one of your own puffles to play with. If you don't have one, a red puffle will play with you. Use the spacebar to launch your puffle into action.

Build a Cannon
The main object of the game is to collect Puffle O's with your puffle to build a cannon, piece by piece. To collect these tasty treats, you'll have to steer your puffle through the sky using your arrow keys. You will master the game once you have all of the pieces of your cannon.

Use Strategy

There are cannons and balloons in the sky that can help you change the direction of your puffle or send it flying higher. But watch out for obstacles such as floating pianos and cactus plants. They'll send your puffle reeling!

All players can play the Blue Sky version of this game. If you are a member and you complete Blue Sky, you can play Soda Sunset. When you complete Soda Sunset, you're ready to play the final version, Box Dimension.

Aim for the Flames

Send your puffle flying through the flaming hoop to get through each level of the game. Collect as many Puffle O's as possible before you leave each level.

A Crabby Foe

On some levels you will encounter a crab who tries to stop you from completing each level.

Stamp Book

Speedy Stamps
You can earn five Stamps for getting through levels and obstacles quickly.

Get Crabby
Earn Stamps by defeating the crabs.

Cannon rewards
Earn Stamps when you build and upgrade your cannon.

Game Spotlight: Puffle Rescue

The underground Mine can be a dangerous place, especially if you're a puffle. In this game, you can help out by rescuing puffles who are stuck in the Mine and can't get out. To play, enter the Mine Shaft and check out the bulletin board. Then click on the puffle you want to rescue.

How to Play:
Choose Your Adventure

If you choose the blue puffle, you'll be hopping across the ice to save it. If you're a member, you can rescue the pink or the black puffles. The pink puffles are trapped in the underground mine tunnels, and the black puffles are underwater.

If you complete the black puffle game, you'll receive a key to a secret underwater room!

Move Carefully

Use your arrow keys to jump from one ice block to another, hop on a mine cart, or swim. Your goal is to get to each puffle and bring it back to the start square. Make sure whatever you're landing on is sturdy, or you may fall.

Watch Out for Creatures

Some creatures in the game are helpful: I've observed that bats in the pink puffle mode will pick you up and drop you where you need to go. In the black puffle game, a giant squid will lead you to a secret underwater room. But watch out for sharks in the blue puffle game and orange octopi in the black puffle game. They'll zap you!

Stamp Book

You can earn 27 Stamps in Puffle Rescue for speed, finding gold, and rescuing puffles.

Game Spotlight: Thin Ice

This game stars a black puffle who's so fired up that he melts blocks of ice. You can find this arcade-style game in the Dance Lounge on the second floor of the Night Club.

How to Play
Move the Puffle
Use your arrow keys to move the puffle from the start to the end of the maze. Every time the puffle passes over an ice tile it will melt, and you won't be able to go back over it.

There is a secret room hidden on Level 19. To get there, look for a false wall in the top right corner of the maze.

Collect Coins and Keys
Look for bags of coins and keys and plan your route so that you pass over them. In some mazes you'll need a key so that you can get to the exit.

RESET   POINTS 753

Melt Every Tile

In many mazes you can easily get from the start to the finish. The trick to earning points (and Stamps) is to try to melt every tile in the maze successfully. Take your time and plan out your path.

> **When you're in the Dance Lounge, be sure to check out the neon puffles on the walls.**

Move Blocks

In some mazes you'll find solid blocks that won't melt when you pass over them. Move them correctly and you'll be able to reach difficult areas of the maze.

Stamp Book

Earn Stamps in this game when you collect coin bags, find the hidden room, melt ice tiles, move blocks, and master all of the mazes.

Game Spotlight: Puffle Roundup

I've spent many hours in the wild studying puffles, and one thing I know is that they're not easy to catch! It takes a lot of patience and skill. In this game, you can practise herding wild puffles. Head to the Pet Shop and click on the Employees Only door to get started.

Some penguins say that red puffles are the fastest and hardest to catch.

How to Play
Move Your Mouse
Your goal is to get all of the puffles into the pen. Move your mouse around them to lead them in the right direction. To get your puffle to move down the screen, put your mouse above it. Put your mouse below a puffle to get it to move up the screen.

Watch for Strays

Some puffles will try to escape into the wilderness. The more puffles you herd, the more points you get, so it's worth it to try and go after them.

CAUGHT: 0
ESCAPED: 0

91

Build Up Speed

The faster you round up puffles, the more coins you'll earn. When you're first learning the game, it's smart to start out slow. But try to get faster with practice to rack up more gold.

Tip: Try herding your puffles into a group first before herding them into the pen.

Meet Some Famous Puffles

I think every puffle is special in its own way. But there are some puffles on the island who have captured the attention of penguins. Some, like Yarr and Lolz, are the loyal companions of famous penguins. Others, like the Keeper of the Boiler Room, can always be found in the same place. And some of them are puffles that I trained to work with the Elite Penguin Force - the EPF.

The Elite Puffles first appeared in the Nintendo DS game Club Penguin: Elite Penguin Force.

The Elite Puffles

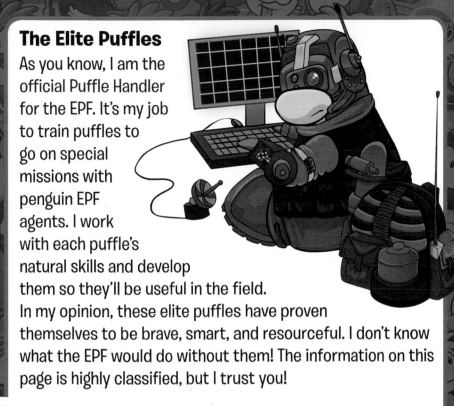

As you know, I am the official Puffle Handler for the EPF. It's my job to train puffles to go on special missions with penguin EPF agents. I work with each puffle's natural skills and develop them so they'll be useful in the field.

In my opinion, these elite puffles have proven themselves to be brave, smart, and resourceful. I don't know what the EPF would do without them! The information on this page is highly classified, but I trust you!

Most of the elite puffles were featured in a book called Puffle Pals Adventures: Music Makes Magic, which has appeared in the Book Room during holiday parties.

Just Whistle

When I train puffles for the EPF, I use a whistle to teach them commands. An agent can use a whistle to call a puffle to his or her side in an emergency.

Did You Know?

Each of the Elite Puffles is featured on a Card-Jitsu card.

Famous Puffles: Red

Yarr

When Captain Rockhopper discovered one particular red puffle, he quickly became good friends with him. The pirate penguin asked this puffle to become first mate of the Migrator, and the puffle accepted. Every time Rockhopper called out "Yarr!", the puffle came hopping toward him, and that's how he got his name.

When Rockhopper docks his ship on Club Penguin, he'll take Yarr with him when they walk around the island. You can also find Yarr hanging out in the ship's tall crow's nest, shooting snowballs out of his cannon.

Catch Up with Yarr

Captain Rockhopper used to keep a journal of his adventures with Yarr. You can find the journal in the Book Room on the second floor of the Coffee Shop. In the back of the journal is a key to the Captain's Quarters. When the Migrator docks, use the key to visit Rockhopper's quarters. Now he posts stories and news on his Notice Board. There you can find interesting news about Yarr. Once, Rockhopper posted that he wanted to get Yarr his own silver surfboard.

Blast

This Elite Puffle is an expert at shooting himself out of a cannon, like other red puffles. But I've trained Blast to increase his speed and accuracy so that he can crash through heavy objects. Blast wears a helmet when he's in action to make sure he doesn't get hurt.

Famous Puffles: Green
Keeper of the Boiler Room

If you've ever been in the Night Club, you've probably seen a happy green puffle dancing and bouncing on top of the big speaker closest to the stairs. Penguins have often wondered about this puffle, who almost never leaves its perch above the dance floor. Who is this mysterious puffle and what is its job?

A Hidden Passage

This green puffle has become known as "The Keeper of the Boiler Room". The Boiler Room lies underneath the Night Club, and from this building the only way to get down there is through a secret entrance. It's in the speaker to the right of the DJ booth. Because the green puffle is always facing this secret entrance, penguins have assumed it's there to guard the entrance to the Boiler Room.

A Haunted Past

If you go into the Book Room on the second floor of the Coffee Shop, you'll find a book called Truth or Dare. This book tells the story of two penguins, RodgerRodger and DanielD, who are frightened by strange noises in the Boiler Room. They're sure it's a ghost, but when they investigate, they discover that a green puffle is to blame—the same puffle that bounces on the speaker.

Be sure to visit this green puffle during the annual Halloween Party. It's usually wearing a special mask for the event.

Flit

This Elite Puffle can fly with the help of his red-and-white propeller hat. Green puffles are natural flyers, so I've trained Flit to fly and grab objects that penguin agents can't reach. Flit can also fly much faster than ordinary puffles.

Famous Puffles: Pink

Loop

When I was training Loop to become an Elite Puffle, I noticed how skilled she was with her jump rope. That gave me an idea, and I taught Loop how to use the jump rope as a lasso. Loop can swing her lasso and use it to grab fast-moving objects.

Loop likes using her lasso so much that she gets into the spirit by wearing a cowboy hat when she swings it.

Flare wears a blue welding mask when he's working.

Famous Puffles: Black
Flare

In the wild, the ability of a black puffle to burst into flame can sometimes get out of hand. When I was training Flare, I had to find a way to control that fiery power. Uncontrolled fire can be dangerous, but heat also has the power to warm us... and to create.

Then it hit me–Flare could use his powers to become an expert welder! I knew that the ability to weld and repair metal would come in handy out in the field, when EPF gear can easily break down, or when agents encounter booby traps. Flare quickly picked up the skill, and now he can shoot a precise blue flame from his mouth when he welds.

A fiery black puffle is the star of the Thin Ice video game. Turn to page 56 to find out more.

Famous Puffles: Blue

Bouncer

Blue puffles love to throw snowballs, so I knew exactly what I needed to do when I was training Bouncer. After countless hours of target practice, Bouncer can now throw snowballs with amazing speed and accuracy. And because Bouncer is so loyal, you know that you can count on her to come through in any situation.

When Bouncer throws snowballs, she wears a winter beanie to keep her head warm.

Famous Puffles: Purple

Lolz

Everyone knows that purple puffles are great dancers, so it makes sense that this purple puffle is a constant companion to Cadence, the DJ at the Night Club. Cadence also runs the Dance Contest game.

Cadence first appeared with Lolz at the 2011 Puffle Party, when penguins saw Cadence walking her around the island. Lolz appears on Cadence's player card with a blue streak in her fur, matching her owner's dyed hair.

Pop

Pop is an Elite Puffle with a very special ability: she can blow amazingly strong, huge bubbles capable of lifting and moving heavy objects. Pop's bubble-blowing powers have gotten EPF agents out of trouble more than once.

Famous Puffles: Yellow

Chirp

Yellow puffles are naturally musical, so when I trained this Elite Puffle I focused on her ability to play the flute. Now Chirp can play a variety of tones so high and so loud that they can do amazing things. Chirp's flute tones can break through a wall of ice without damaging what's inside, or short-circuit the motor of a jet pack to stop a villain from getting away.

Chirp wears a beret when she plays the flute.

Keeper of the Stage

This yellow puffle first showed up when the Stage was being built. Now it appears in all of the plays. To see it, click on the yellow lever on the Switchbox 3000.

The Ringmaster

Every year, the puffles perform a circus during the Fall Fair. This cute yellow puffle, with its moustache and top hat, acts as ringmaster.

Famous Puffles: White

Chill

Chill is the newest member of the Elite Puffles. He has an amazing ability to control and work with ice. If there's a stick of dynamite about to explode, Chill can freeze it with one breath. He can also create things out of ice, like a sled so an agent can make a quick escape down a mountainside. He can also join things together by freezing them, such as broken parts of a machine. I have a feeling that we'll be seeing a lot more of what Chill and his icy breath can do.

Who'll Be Next?

So far, there aren't any famous orange or brown puffles on Club Penguin. But I'm training two puffles who may fill the gap! Can you help me name them? Use your imagination!

Name

....

....

....

Famous for

....

....

....

....

Make a Puffle

Puffles are special and unique to Club Penguin, but you can make your own mini one in a few easy steps! Before you get started, make sure to ask an adult for help.

What You Will Need:
- Pom-pom balls in your favourite puffle colours (any size)
- Glue
- Googly eyes
- Black felt

Step 1:
Get all of your supplies and lay them on paper towel or newspaper to protect your surface from glue. Choose a coloured pom-pom in your favourite puffle colour, or invent a new one!

Step 2:
Glue the googly eyes on the centre of the pom-pom ball. Make sure they're spaced evenly apart and are glued on well so that they don't fall off! Allow the glue to dry before moving on to Step 3.

Step 3:

Now that your puffle has eyes, it's time to give it a smile. Cut out a smile shape from your black felt - make it as thin as you can. Glue the smile on underneath your googly eyes. Again, make sure it's glued on well!

You've just made your own puffle! The fun part about this is you can make as many puffles as you want. Keep making mini puffles and you can have your own puffle party!

Make Your Own Puffle Hat

You and your puffle can dress alike with these hat crafts! Be sure to ask an adult for help before getting started.

Princess Cap

Step 1: Roll the piece of cardboard into a cone shape the size of your head. Use a piece of tape to hold it shut. Try the hat on your head – you may have to adjust the size.

Step 2: Once you've got the right size, tape the hat completely closed and trim off any uneven edges.

Step 3: You can leave your hat plain or decorate it by gluing on the plastic gems or making designs with the glitter glue. Allow to dry completely.

Step 4: Tape a piece of ribbon to the top of the hat so that it falls down the back.

Step 5: Put the hat on and measure to see how long a piece of string or elastic you'll need to fit under your chin. Cut the string or elastic to the right size, and then use a stapler to secure the ends to the sides of the cone. Your princess hat is finished!

What You Will Need:

A large piece of pink cardboard
Scissors
Tape
Plastic gems or glitter glue (optional)
Ribbon
String or elastic
Stapler

Pirate Hat

What You Will Need:
1 sheet of coloured paper

Step 1: Start with the sheet of paper laid out in front of you so the shorter sides are on the top and bottom.

Step 2: Fold the top of the paper down to the bottom, folding the sheet in half. You will now have a long rectangle in front of you.

Step 3: Fold the top left corner to the centre of the page.

Step 4: Fold the top right corner to the centre of the page.

Step 5: Fold the bottom top flap up a few inches to where the corners meet. This will create the brim of your hat. Make sure to use only the top layer of newspaper.

Step 6: Turn over the paper hat. Fold the bottom flap only to create the back brim of your hat. You're finished! Your pirate hat is ready to wear.

How To Draw a Puffle

Let a puffle be the star of your very own artistic masterpiece! Follow these steps and you'll be drawing puffles like a pro.

1. It all starts with a circle. It doesn't have to be perfect! Draw a small circle to begin.

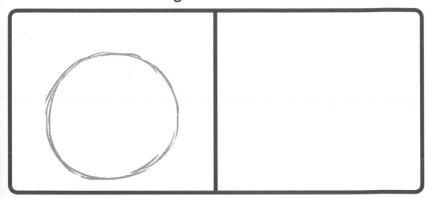

2. Lightly draw a line down the side of the circle, as shown. This line shows you where your puffle will be facing, and where you will place its eyes and smile! Then draw another line from left to right across the middle of the circle.

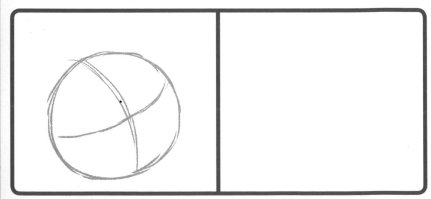

3. Puffles have big, cute eyes. Draw two kinds of squashed circles as shown below.

Underneath the eyes will be your puffle's mouth. To make the mouth, draw two lines that are on top of one another in a smiling shape, and connect them to a point at the corner of the mouth.

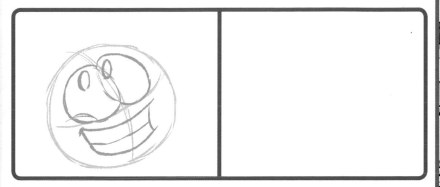

4. To give your puffle hair, begin at the top of the circle, and draw a zigzag line floating slightly above the circle.

5. Up until now, the lighter lines you have drawn are called guidelines. Now you can add the detail lines on top of your guidelines. These lines are darker. To make them, go over the important lines you drew with a darker pencil or marker. Now your puffle is complete!

Answers to Your Tough Puffle Questions

Whenever I meet other puffle owners, I'm always asked lots of questions. I've answered some of the most popular ones for you here.

What food should I feed my puffle? There are so many choices!

Different puffles prefer different types of food, so try everything from cheese to Puffle O's and see which your puffle likes best. We all know that carrots are better for you than cake, but a treat every now and then can't hurt!

I fed my puffle but it's still not happy. What should I do?

Check the stat bars on your puffle's page. The yellow bars will tell you if your puffle needs grooming, playtime, or sleep.

Why do puffles run away?

A puffle will run away if it has not been cared for in a long time. Visit your igloo every time you play, and take care of your puffle.

Why can't my puffle use all of the toys I bought for it?

Puffles are like penguins–they have unique personalities. You might love to play soccer but don't love to dance, for example. Well, your puffle is the same. It will play with the things it likes best.

No matter what I do, my black puffle always looks unhappy. What's wrong?

Black puffles aren't really grumpy . . . they're just a little intense. Try letting it play with its skateboard. You may just see it smile!

Congratulations!

If you've made it to the end of this book, that means you know an awful lot about puffles! Nice job. But this doesn't mean that your puffle journey is over.

I've been studying puffles for a long time. The more I learn about them, the more I realize I have a lot left to learn. There is still so much we don't know about these friendly creatures.

So keep playing with your puffles and taking good care of them. Curl up together with the Club Penguin Times and check for news about puffles. Read the Club Penguin blog. These are all great ways to become even more of a puffle expert!